Unstoppable Entrepreneurship
Text and photos copyright © Ilkka O. Lavas
2014 Sundea Publishing Finland LavasDesign Ltd
ISBN 978-952-68264-0-0

Publishing Editor: Jukka Niemelä / Prepsikka Ltd
Cover photo: Alicia Miller / 99designs.com
Back cover photo: Arto Ketola
Design: SaaraLiu / Saara Liukkonen

Written with a Samsung Galaxy S2 in Cambodia, China,
Thailand, Spain, Russia, USA, in an airplane somewhere,
and in Finland. Translated by the author in California, USA.

"Attitude! Now we're at the core of success and 'unstoppability' – in decision making and having the guts to set milestones and goals for yourself. Goals are incredibly often realised, so be careful what you wish for!"

    Taneli Tikka, Serial Entrepreneur

"A young serial entrepreneur's valuable experiences for startups and anyone interested in entrepreneurship. This book is inspirational and brings hope for the future. You can learn from the experiences of others – you don't have to make the same mistakes that others have made."

    Eero Lehti, honoured businessman

"This book is full of inspiration and encouragement for entrepreneurs and the entrepreneurially minded. The reading experience is enjoyable and it really makes you think about your habits. It brings a fresh and inspiring perspective to entrepreneurship."

    Ulla Vilkman, HR Teacher and Managing Director

Unstoppable Entrepreneurship

Text and pictures copyright © Ilkka O. Lavas
2014 Sundea Publishing Finland LavasDesign Ltd
ISBN 978-952-68264-0-0

Publishing editor: Jukka Niemelä, Prepsikka Oy
Cover picture: Alicia Miller, 99designs.com
Back cover photo: Arto Ketola
Design: SaaraLiu / Saara Liukkonen

Written with a Samsung Galaxy S2 in Cambodia, China,
Thailand, Spain, Russia, USA, in an airplane somewhere,
and in Finland. Translated by the author in California, USA.

Contents

Never Give Up

My friend has cancer. A liver tumour causes him chronic, severe pain and pressure. He told me how hard it is to live in constant pain. It's difficult to sleep, and yet he doesn't have the strength to stay awake because the pain relievers makes him so exhausted. And it doesn't matter if he sits or stands – there's no comfortable position for him.

But my friend fights this cancer, even though he's under constant care. He had to accept his situation and give his life over to his doctor's hands – to have the courage to ask for help. Near the end of his care programme, a large part of his liver was removed, leaving only a small part left to live with. Soon after his care was completed, he started feeling better. His doctors couldn't remove all of the cancer because it was so widely spread, and gave him half a year to live – one year, max.

Well, he was still alive and fighting half a year after doctors thought he would be dead. He didn't let cancer control his life. He accepted the pain. He accepted that in time, his doctors would increase the pain medicine's dosage so much that he could no longer drive a car. And he accepted that each increase in dosage meant that he had even less time to live his life with meaning.

If you can't change the situations in your life, accept that. Ask for help. Change what you can, but accept the things that are not possible for you to change.

My friend is unstoppable. He wants to live even though he knows he doesn't have much time. He wants to help other people, especially his friends. He says that even as his death grows closer, he will never give up.

In these rare moments when we realise we're not immortal and we're truly going to die one day, we often start to see our lives in a different light. We prioritise things differently when these situations arise and give us pause. Sometimes we need another person in our lives or an accident to make us stop and think about how we live our lives.

But you don't need to wait for life's crises – you can prioritise important things in your life at any time. Taking time to reflect on your life is a very important task, and everyone should make time for life planning regularly. Some people set goals and priorities frequently, while others do it only when there are no other options.

Anyone can be unstoppable by taking control of their life.

You are unstoppable when you are the master of your own life. An unstoppable person lives a healthy life style. The unstoppable you loves life, lives for the moment and has dreams. The unstoppable you sets goals and gets closer to your dreams milestone by milestone. Being unstoppable is about failing, being sorry and learning from mistakes. The unstoppable you accepts your own limits and is realistic. Being unstoppable is about having strength, keeping life in balance and possessing what we Finns call "sisu" – an emphatic persistence and perseverance – plus the willingness to live life to the fullest.

You can be unstoppable, if you want to.

Ilkka O. Lavas
New York

You Can Be Unstoppable

Anyone who wants to be unstoppable can be. To do it, you must promote yourself to be the CEO of your own life – to be the boss and in control of you. In other words: you must lead yourself.

I've learned that the better I lead myself, the better I manage my businesses. It took me a long time as an entrepreneur to understand that leading requires regular development discussions. For leaders, development discussions mean pausing for self-reflection. They are discussions with myself or with my mentors.

A leader's most important tasks are to inspire, set goals, measure and cheer on the team. As an entrepreneur you have to be your own boss. You are important. With this book, I hope you'll learn to remember yourself. That you'll learn to see your life in different perspectives and be inspired again and again. I also hope this book encourages you throughout various stages of your career.

If you're not (yet) an entrepreneur, I ask you to consider what entrepreneurship could bring to your everyday life at work. If you're looking toward entrepreneurship as a career choice, I encourage you to give it a chance. Entrepreneurship is worth trying. It's a good choice for many – so long as you don't take a financial risk that's too big to handle. A good level of risk is when you can still keep your head above water, even if the worst-case scenario comes to play. Make sure that you can stay afloat even if your business collapses. And don't keep yourself up at night with worry. An entrepreneur, like anyone else, should take care to get enough sleep.

If you're already an entrepreneur, I hope this book will give you more inspiration for your life. I hope that you'll remember the reasons why you started out as an entrepreneur in the first place. I encourage you to meet colleagues who can help you to survive through difficult times – and friends who enjoy the good times with you.

As you read along, consider how you could become unstoppable in your life. I hope you'll get new ideas and thoughts that bring more energy and power to your entrepreneurship. I hope that you'll find what we Finns call "sisu" – that relentless persistence and perseverance – and the seed of unstoppable power inside you.

I encourage you to treat the challenges in your life as possibilities to learn something new. Learning is about finding joy in your imperfections. Enjoy the great journey we call life.

Life is a fight.
Life is a game.
As an entrepreneur
you know you can be unstoppable.
Crave it. Be brave.
The unstoppable person wins the battle before it
has even started.

What it Takes to
Be Unstoppable

Earlier I discussed what Finns call "sisu". It's an important ingredient to being unstoppable.

Physical and mental health are also a part of what it takes to be unstoppable, as are training, sleep, recharging yourself, recreation, balance in life, and honesty to your very own self.

Being unstoppable is about getting excited, but staying humble. That you never give up. It's about learning from your mistakes and the mistakes of others. It takes crazy amounts of courage and a love of life. It's also about forgiving, asking for forgiveness, and enjoying your success. It's remembering to say thanks, getting appreciated and creating something fresh and new.

In the following chapters I'll give you an in-depth view of what it takes to be unstoppable. These are the secret ingredients to unstoppable entrepreneurship, gathered from my own experiences in entrepreneurship and adventures in life.

Manage your life so it's all in balance. Then you're unstoppable – knowing that you can fail, but can stand on your own two feet again. And you never give up.

Toughing it Through

Even when you're unstoppable, you can still burn out.

When you feel you're being crushed under the pressure of debts and taxes, and you still come out from under it all alive and kicking, you'll know that you are unstoppable. You'll understand what being unstoppable truly means to you.

I've been an entrepreneur since I was 17 years old. At first everything was pleasant, fun and exciting. Later in 2002, I was 23 years old and had just finished my obligatory army service in Finland. The IT bubble had just burst.

Thanks to my army service, I was in good physical condition. My company employed 17 people. When the IT bubble burst, my company's volume of orders fell and we had a serious cash-flow crisis. Things became much less pleasant, fun and exciting.

I couldn't sleep because I was worrying about how I could pay salaries to my employees. I was mentally burned out. I crashed. In fact, I almost went crazy. I had to make a choice between two bad choices: should I file my company for bankruptcy, or should I try to continue the business? I honestly didn't want bankruptcy, so I thought about the latter option.

I didn't want to give up. So I started thinking – what is the worst thing that can happen to me if I fail trying to save this company? Well, I realised the answer was option one, bankruptcy. Regardless if I failed at saving the company, or didn't even try saving it, the worst-case scenario was that my company would go bankrupt. Luckily, my own house was not collateral on my company debts, so my own private property was protected. I calculated that I could save the company by downsizing the amount of employees and by handling all the sold, but still open, cases well.

I called the tax officer and made a deal about the payment terms. One of the debtors took some of our office furniture as payment for their bills. With a heavy heart, I had to lay off 12 people, including some very good friends and my son's godfather. I saved wherever possible. I couldn't even pay my own salary for many months.

This challenging downsizing period finally ended 14 months later, when I paid the last unpaid tax payment. The pen dropped from my hand to the floor. I was exhausted. But I didn't give up. I survived my first big business challenge. It was difficult – a real-life course in "Business and Economy University".

In high school we didn't have courses called "How to lay people off" or "How to survive and manage a cash crisis". Still, my business survived without these kinds of courses. And I continued on as an entrepreneur despite this challenge. I gave entrepreneurship a second chance. To this day, my business-survival experience gives me the courage to take on new challenges. Everything will always be all right in the end, and if it's not all right, it doesn't mean it's the end.

Those that risk nothing and do nothing get nothing.

Being unstoppable requires a never-give-up attitude.

It also requires conscious actions: regular self-reflection, self-management, development and leading others.

You are unstoppable when you face challenges and perceive them as opportunities to learn something new.

Protect yourself financially and don't take risks too big to handle.

While reading this book, remind yourself why you do the job you do. What is your mission and what is your company's mission? Think about how you lead yourself and how you lead others.

You only have one life, so live it!

The Unstoppable Entrepreneur Has "Sisu"

Being unstoppable means you have Finnish "sisu" at your core. Sisu means taking action against the odds and displaying courage and determination in the face of adversity. It's about deciding on a course of action, then sticking to that decision despite repeated failures. Some people feel that sisu also implies a bit of madness – the type of reckless sense of adventure that inspires a person to take on something in the face of incredible odds.

Sisu is the secret ingredient of life that empowers entrepreneurs. I've spoken with thousands of entrepreneurs and noticed that it's true – entrepreneurs have special superpowers! They have sisu, along with good habits. And they also have a crazy sense of adventure when it comes to taking on risks. That makes them unstoppable.

As an entrepreneur I love helping people so much that it doesn't make sense – one might even call it a bit "crazy". I love it when my customers thrive and grow. I love that more than my own achievements. Their successes make my own life important and successful.

I'm also super enthusiastic about my work and don't even count the hours spent there. I enjoy it when people at work feel good and achieve their goals, plus our goals together.

When my company almost went bankrupt 12 years ago, it was a huge challenge for me. And yet – it was an awesome experience. I wouldn't change any of it because I learned so much from that turnaround.

Entrepreneurship is about living life with the pros and cons. Sometimes you enjoy success. Sometimes you learn from your mistakes and failures. As an entrepreneur, you accept life has its good days and its bad. Sometimes life makes you angry. Sometimes it makes you cry. Sometimes you'll jump for joy. A happy and full life embraces all types of feelings and life adventures.

#1 Make Plans to Improve 12 Times Per Year

The unstoppable entrepreneur iterates and wants to perpetually improve. Changes can be assessed more easily when you make them and measure results once per month. To develop personally, you need to be aware of and accept what you should change. When asked about the secret recipe behind his band Apulanta's success, successful Finnish musician Toni Wirtanen says, "You should never stop and be happy with the current situation. You will always find something to fix or to learn".

I've set a reminder on my calendar 12 times per year on the very last day of every month. That's when I sit with my notes and examine if I've been doing the things I decided I wanted to do, and check if I've achieved the milestones I set for myself. I also reflect on my life by making a list of things that would improve my companies or my life.

Sometimes I find things I don't want to do and I consider if I even have to do those things. I also find things that I have to concentrate on more. When it comes to the big questions, I ask for help and opinions from my friends and mentors.

If you want to be unstoppable, devote time to making improvement plans 12 times per year. Check where you're at and what you've been doing. Go someplace where you can be alone with your thoughts. Think about what you could change in your own behaviour or company processes.

If meditative monologue is not your thing, ask someone to be your mental trainer. I guarantee you'll find someone who wants to help you in life. He or she can be a friend, fellow, business angel, business mentor or colleague. All you need to do is ask for help.

#2 It's OK to Be a Little Bit Crazy

The unstoppable entrepreneur is brave and a little bit crazy. Courage, combined with an ability to take risks, brings new opportunities to learn and great new adventures with infinite possibilities.

To become unstoppable, you also need the courage to start a business and the possibility to be successful. On the other hand, the unstoppable entrepreneur accepts the risk of possible failure.

I've been a part of many successful businesses. Looking back, many of those ventures have been very risky. But if all I had seen were the risks in advance, I wouldn't have had the courage to go into business.

IKEA founder Ingvar Kamprad said that we sometimes talk so much about the risks and idea of failure, that we forget reality. Analysing things too deeply may kill a great idea before it's even out of the design phase.

In my best successes, I've trusted my intuition and business sense, and the possibility to play things by ear. A good business will develop along the way.

The bigger the success, the bigger the risks you usually have to take. Choose an appropriate challenge, and face each of them one at a time. Analyse enough, but not too much. If you want success, give it a chance to happen.

#3 Build a Network Around You

The difference between an unstoppable person and the rest is the network they've built.

When I started my businesses, I had my first client, but no idea of how to run a business. I didn't know anything about bookkeeping or invoicing. I didn't have a clue about what taxes I needed to pay. But my friend had a bookkeeping company, so I called him to help out. He did and I learned.

In my early years as an entrepreneur, I met a consultant who said you should keep personal records of the people you've done business with or have been in touch with. At the time I thought this made no sense – of course I would remember everyone I've met and done business with. But something about that lecture was compelling. I was familiar with the theory that every person knows each other through six other people. So I decided to give what the consultant suggested a try.

After a couple of years, I noticed that people I had met earlier in company #1 were now in new positions in some other companies. The theory proved to be true and my network kept growing.

I'm now involved with several organisations, including charity and business networking, which are very valuable to entrepreneurs. While networking, you get to know other active people who may be valuable to your business one day – or you could be valuable to them.

When I completed the manuscript for this book, I contacted the people and entrepreneurs I respect most. Some of them I've met through entrepreneur organisations, and others elsewhere. I got a lot of help from them to write this book. Maybe if I hadn't started building a network 15 years ago already, this book would not have even been published. It could very well be that without help from my networks, I couldn't have survived downsizing my company 10 years ago. Luckily, I had courage to ask for help and had created a supportive network of people around me.

Network with people who can be successful with you. Find mentors, employees and partners you can ask for help when you need it. And help your people when they need help.

Reflect on Your Own Life and Habits

When I saw myself reflected in the mirror,
I noticed how messed up my hair was.
I felt ashamed because
I had porridge smeared across my cheek
and my shirt collars were still turned up.

We all have this sort of problem –
we scrutinise and try to change others,
while instead we should start with ourselves.

The unstoppable you reflects
on your own thoughts, habits and soul,
and asks others to help with that reflection.

#4 Decide What You Want to Be When You Grow Up

An unstoppable entrepreneur knows what they're going to be when they "grow up". Being unstoppable also means knowing you can change this decision at any time.

After downsizing my company from 2002 – 2003, I felt crushed and defeated. I decided I never wanted to be in the IT-field again, and I no longer wanted to be an entrepreneur. I shifted my focus and began studying management and started working on an MBA.

My MBA studies began with personal development and self-reflection. The first homework I got was to answer a few questions:

• What do I want to do? (Dreams)
• What don't I want to do? (Don'ts)
• What I am good? (Strengths)
• What am I bad at? (Weaknesses)
• Where do I have opportunities to improve? (Opportunity scenarios).

I looked at many job postings, but none interested me. The jobs that interested me were in the IT-field. I found myself rethinking my earlier decision. I'm good at IT-related things and I really love the field. Plus I didn't find any interesting jobs, so I decided to try again as an entrepreneur.

What it comes down to is this – I stopped to think, but I didn't stop. I understood that downsizing my company was a very important life lesson and through that experience I learned things I would never learn at school. In the future I would be stronger, more experienced, wiser and able to react quickly in changing business markets.

Taking that time to pause and ponder was an important moment in my life. Just when I was ready to give up everything I had been hanging on to, I was able to choose from scratch where I wanted to go and what I wanted from my life.

Choose what kind of life's riches you want. How much money and love? What kind of friends do you want to hang with? Do you want to live a healthy life? What do you want to mean to other people? Stop and examine yourself. Find your strengths and weaknesses.

Get to know what you want to do and think about what your customers would like to buy. Consider if there's something missing in this world that you could provide – something that's easy for you to do exceptionally well, but difficult for your competitors to provide.

Take a few minutes to stop and consider these things for yourself:

I am good at _____ and _____ and _____.
I want to be in the _____-industry
as a _____(in which position),
because _____(why?).
I would like to try what it would feel like to be in
_____-industry
_____(doing what),
because_____(why?).
When I "grow up", I'm going to
be_____.

My dream day in 5 or 10 years starts in the morning and ends at night, and this is how it goes and what I feel:

_____
_____
_____.

When I die, people remember these things about me:

_____
_____.

23

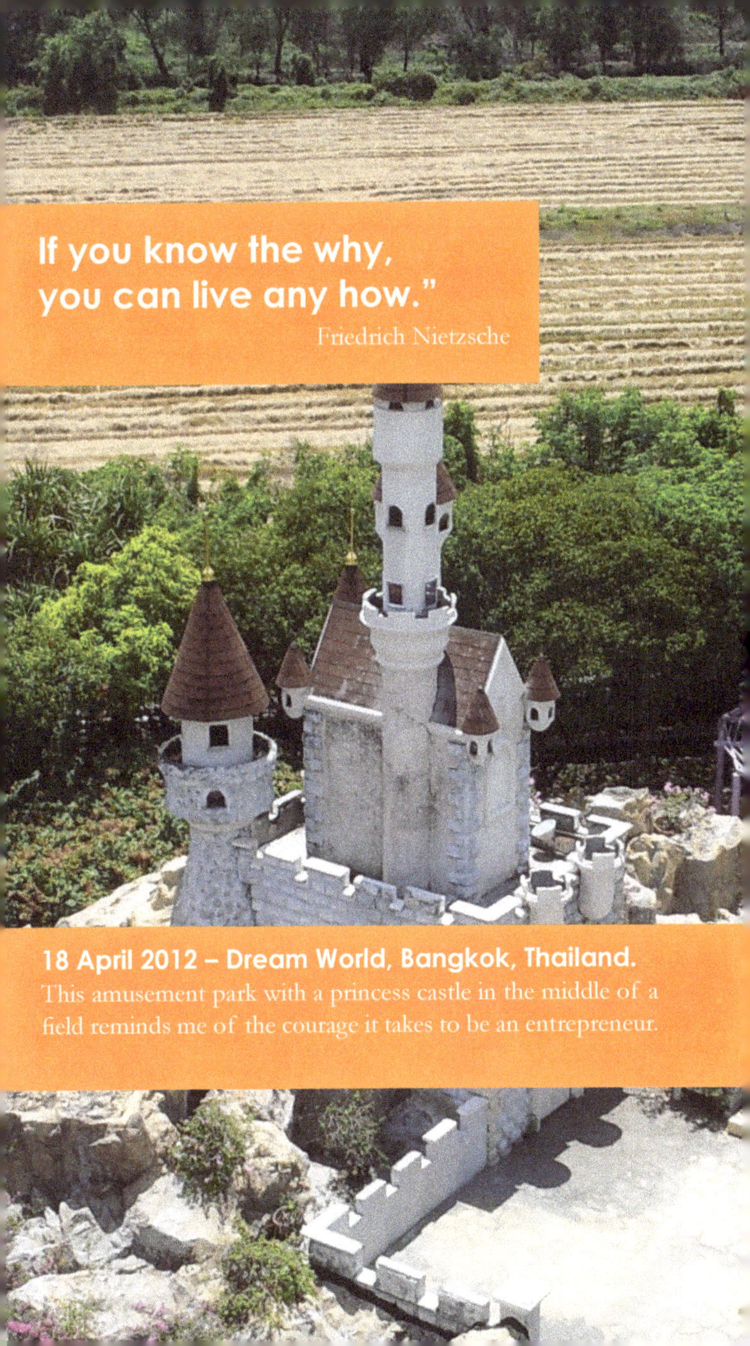

> If you know the why,
> you can live any how."
>
> Friedrich Nietzsche

18 April 2012 – Dream World, Bangkok, Thailand.
This amusement park with a princess castle in the middle of a field reminds me of the courage it takes to be an entrepreneur.

#5 Give Entrepreneurship a Chance

Being unstoppable means leading your own life. Many unstoppable people are entrepreneurs – others are employees but act in an entrepreneurial way.

I was once working for another company than my own. I did my job and did it in an entrepreneurial way. Even when I was a software developer, I created new products and innovations for the company. I wanted to learn new things and developed myself. But eventually I wanted to take on more risk and have more freedom, so I quit my day job and started out as an entrepreneur.

You can be unstoppable while working for others, as a partner, or as an entrepreneur. Some people start off as an entrepreneur for a particular reason, and some people just want to get away from something.

The many reasons to become an entrepreneur

For meaning and to create value:
- you want to help your customers be successful
- you want to create better jobs
- you want to fulfil your dreams
- you want to do things differently
- you want to achieve success, whatever way it means to you
- to get into a business industry of your dreams
- to do things your own way

To get away:
- you want out of your current work
- you want to get out of unemployment
- you hate bureaucracy

Just getting away may motivate you for a short time, but if you want to be successful, you really need to start creating value and meaning for others.

Creating value for others and living a meaningful life mean that you start setting goals for your business and yourself.

I started my first business after I got my first order. Later, I had to rethink the reasons why I'm an entrepreneur. What do I want to do next? What goals will I set in my life? How do I double my earnings in the next five years?

Give entrepreneurship a chance to change your life. Innovate and develop. Plan your entrepreneurial career.

#6 Be a Fighter

The unstoppable entrepreneur believes that what doesn't kill you makes you stronger. Singer Kelly Clarkson would add: "What does not kill you, makes you a fighter."

I've learned to take life as it comes – that every challenge I face has meaning. If I'm hit somewhere once, the next time that place will be stronger. I rise up and develop mentally as a person when I meet challenges head on. I might even say that the challenges have lifted me more than my good experiences.

Don't be afraid of challenges. A high jumper doesn't just quit when they drop the bar. Instead they try again, determined to jump even higher to get over it. Improve. Be a fighter!

Life is challenge – live it.

Huai Yat, Thailand 4 April 2012.

During my time in Huai Yai, I wrote about choosing a path and being brave. Creativity coaches say that you should try to do things in a way you would not normally do them. While I was travelling, I found an odd-looking shortcut that took me to the next stop in half the time than following the asphalt road. The shortcut was scary, but when I got myself into the adventure, I noticed that it was more fun and faster than main road.

#7 Be Curious and Think Differently

The unstoppable entrepreneur is interested in many things. They see how they can change their current processes everywhere, and find alternate business models and improvements.

I've always had varied interests. I believe there's a small philosopher inside of me. I want to understand how things and companies work and why one business does things in a particular way.

When I was a kid, I dissected all sorts of electronic equipment to see how things worked. I do the same nowadays, but with company incomes, processes and expenses. I want to understand why some businesses work, while others do not. I've learned that many businesses can be renovated so long as you take good care of them. I also believe that some businesses are impossible to fix. Even when a business is beyond repair, you can rebuild the whole business again, but that also requires redefining everything starting from the business model to its mission and people.

When you're curious, you're unable to accept that change is impossible. You won't accept it when someone says there are no other options. You will never believe it when they say nothing can be done.

Economists who research decision-making processes say that decision makers with more available options are more efficient than those who are unable to see multiple options. If you have only a few options, the best may not be among those.

Seek out options where others can't seem to find them. And explore options that may, at first glance, seem impossible.

"Life is an adventure –
dare it."
Mother Theresa

18 April 2012 – Dream World Bangkok, Thailand.
While in Dream World, I wrote about sisu, dreaming and courage.

#8 Have Dreams with a Deadline

When the unstoppable entrepreneur dreams, it helps their sub-conscious mind make small decisions and direction changes autonomously. The unstoppable entrepreneur will understand that dreaming helps you achieve your vision, but you also need to take action. Being unstoppable means you're able to find new ways to start doing work.

I've often dreamed about goals that I didn't dare tell others. Even these secret dreams have helped me improve things that will take me step-by-step closer to my goals.

Dreaming is important, but it's just as important to define a schedule. Big innovators are dreamers with a deadline.

Life is a dream. Only you can take yourself to your own life goals. Give your dreams a chance to happen and define a time-line of how you can make them come true.

#9 You Already Have All the Ingredients for Success

Unstoppable entrepreneurship is about being successful the way you define it. Most people today would accept that artists like Picasso, Hemingway or Dali were successful. But people of Picasso's era, for example, argued about the value of his work. Some people thought he was successful, while others thought he didn't understand anything about art.

Have you ever thought that successful people and celebrities are just normal people like you and me? They have some of the same kinds of challenges, life situations and growing pains as we have. Even celebrities experience love, joy and sadness.

Who is successful anyway? Anyone can be successful. You can be too! Being successful depends on how you define your successes and how you live your life. Do you think Picasso cared if anyone thought he was unsuccessful? I believe he was more interested in how he felt about himself. I don't think Picasso painted to be a success. Rather, he painted because he felt compelled to do what he loved and painting was his way to thrive.

No one is more wonderful than anybody else. A "successful" person isn't any more wonderful than a "normal" person. Being unstoppable means you understand that we are all normal, wonderful people and that anyone can be successful. You have the golden key to success in your hands if you want to use it. Yes, you have it! Don't let your thoughts limit your potential – don't be the biggest obstacle to your own success. Live your life to the fullest and use the promise you have within.

Moreover, "normal" people can also be successful without even knowing it themselves. Many celebrities we admire wish they could sometimes be like "normal" people, without notoriety and paparazzis chasing them around. They might dream of times where they don't have to think carefully about everything they say. How much do you think Justin Bieber or Dr. Phil would pay to be like "normal" people just for a day? To walk down the street without fans asking for autographs or help, enjoying anonymous life just like the rest of us. Sometimes we might dream of fame, but those in the public eye know that life and partying without daily scrutiny in the media is more relaxed and free.

I was listening to the radio one day while my colleague Teemu Arina was discussing success. Through the conversation, they discovered new ways of how people define success in their life. An important point touched on in the discussion was how success is often only defined by people who think someone is successful.

I define success differently for myself than you do. That's the best part of being successful.

On Facebook, I asked my friends what success means to people. These were some of their responses:

- Happiness. Meaningfulness. Fellows and Friends.
- I feel success in my life when I make others feel good and they feel it so strongly that they want to return the feeling in kind. <3
- Peace of mind and health. Good friends and great family. Work that provides enough challenge, but not too much stress.
- Success is about having a great time in your own life. We all have to be brave enough to admit to ourselves what makes our lives great (and to not just be like the others). And yes it's important to work for what's important in your life and what makes life good for yourself. Easy. :)
- Knowing that you can make things better with little stake to yourself. For example: creating better services. :)
- Success as an entrepreneur is about creating awesome products that people use and love.
- Money is only the result of something good, not the goal.

As you can see, we define our success differently. How do you define your own success? For one person, it's enough just to be healthy, but someone else may want something more.

Define for yourself what success means to you.

You can be successful when you know what success truly means for you.

My dream is/my dream day goes like this:

_____
_____
_____

For me, being successful means:

1._____
_____
2._____
_____
3._____
_____

These things take me step-by-step toward my dream:

1._____
_____
2._____
_____
3._____
_____

These things will help me realise when I'm successful:

1._____
_____
2._____
_____
3._____
_____

"If you have a dream,
give it a chance to happen."
Richard M. DeVos

Manage Yourself or Someone Else Will

The most important leadership skill is knowing
how to lead yourself.
I'm naturally so lazy that if I don't manage myself,
I can't get anything done.
Successful people do things even when they don't like to if
they know it will take them closer to their dreams.
When you have a choice to make and you don't make it,
that in itself is a choice.
I can only achieve the things I truly want to by managing
myself and my own life goals.
Self-leadership is a skill you can teach yourself.
The unstoppable you can and wants to lead yourself.
Self-management is the key to success that many idle people
keep in their pockets and never use.

#10 The Skill of Self-management

Being unstoppable means you can and will lead yourself. The skill of self-management is important but challenging. It's a paradox. I'm the only one that can push myself to wake up early in the morning to go running. Only I can tell myself to go to sleep early. I'm the only one who can tell myself to get away from the TV and read a book that will help me achieve my goals. No one makes me do anything unless I do it myself.

I can only achieve results by leading myself. Yesterday, I left a party early to go home and sleep because I wanted to wake up early in the morning and write this book – just to delight you! Another night I didn't go out with my friends because I wanted to spend time with my family and children. And as I write this now, my kids are still sleeping, so I have time to write.

I'm not perfect. But I'm always perfect at managing myself. To write this book, I chose a mentor who would follow up on my progress weekly. He listened and gave feedback. I also have a personal trainer to help me keep fit and in good physical condition.

I've read numerous self-management books. As a matter of fact, I read them regularly and buy new ones all the time. Many of these books have the same ideas, but they help me to better understand my life and understand how I see life.

Reflect on how you manage yourself. Do the following tasks. Take a maximum of five minutes out of your life to fill out this list now.

What three things do I want to achieve in my life (goals)?

1. _____
2. _____
3. _____

What milestones do I want to achieve and by when?

1. Milestone: _____
deadline in the end of year ____.
2. Milestone: _____
deadline in the end of year ____.
3. Milestone: _____
deadline in the end of year ____.

I promise myself to get started with these things
(by dd/mm/yy):

1st thing that I will do: _____,
before __ / __ / __.
2nd thing that I will do: _____,
before __ / __ / __.
3rd thing that I will do: _____,
before __ / __ / __.

Who can help me achieve my goals?

Mentor/personal trainer: _____
Mentor/personal trainer: _____

Now put a recurring monthly reminder in your electronic calendar, so you don't forget these important things in your life.

#11 Be Ready to Serve, Anytime

The unstoppable entrepreneur wants to help their customer be successful. You do your work whenever there is business to be done.

When I was in China with some fellow entrepreneurs, I learned that in Chinese culture, the supplier is always ready to serve the customer. If I want to be successful, I can't always count my hours at work. I can't just up and leave at 5 pm, because my customers are always my first priority. I don't mind if a customer calls me on Saturday for an order, because I know it means that my competitor did not get that order.

Unstoppable entrepreneurs may look like workaholics. But I don't think we are. I would rather compare us to top athletes that skip partying for a night to prepare for the world championships.

I stopped watching crap on TV years ago to give myself more time to read and proceed in my career. Prioritising rest is important. If I want to be effective the next day, I leave even the best parties early to go to sleep.

Think about how you could be more effective. What could some acts of self-discipline bring to you? Consider times when you should put the happiness of your customer or environment before your own. What can you drop out of your life to do something more valuable and honourable instead?

#12 Know What You Want

Goal setting

Unstoppable entrepreneurship is about knowing where you want to go. When the ship leaves, the captain knows the destination harbour.

My own milestones can be categorised into short-term goals, in the next hour or day, or long-term goals. Often I forget to set any goals. At the end of the day, I notice that the hours of my workday have just disappeared while doing some task. I feel like I didn't get anything done. That's when I know I need to stop and make changes in my goal-setting habits. I take my calendar and reschedule the rest of my week in a way that I know I'm doing things in the correctly prioritised order. There's a huge difference between doing things right and in **doing right things right.**

Set goals and milestones for yourself. Decide how to use your time. You're not really in a hurry. Choose what's important for today and keep focused on that.

The unstoppable you doesn't sail without goals

I've seen many people in my career doing their work routinely without milestones or targets. That might even be good during a certain stage of your life. I was once in that situation myself.

When there were only a few opportunities available to me, I had to grab a hold of each and every one of them. But my life at that time was like I was sailing at sea without goals. I was just fishing around, not going anywhere. I couldn't choose which direction I should go next. I didn't even want to choose which harbour I should go to next.

For some people at some point in their lives, living as if they're running on a treadmill might be fine. But by end of the week they don't even know where all their time went. For me,

Enjoy your life.

28 March 2012, Phong Pheng, Cambodia.
Motorcycle-adventure entrepreneur Severi Virolainen and
I preparing for a drive to Bokor Mountain in Cambodia.

this way of living will no longer do. Because when you sail the seas of life without goals, you might move around just fine, but you'll never reach your destination.

You want a goal, and you want to know how far you are from that goal. Make a route from where you are to where you want to be and track your progress.

Lifestyle entrepreneur: an adventurer with a goal

My entrepreneur colleague Juha Viitala enjoys mountaineering and travelling around the world. One of his first projects was an around-the-world trip for which he collected money from sponsors. Sponsors paid for his entire journey – an awesome fully financed trip for a young guy!

Travelling became Juha's life. His business model later changed so that his hobby became his work. Juha is now (at the time I wrote this book) a partner for Mandala Travel travel agency. He can travel around the world and is living his dream.

Another friend of mine, Severi Virolainen, is a passionate motorcyclist. I often see on Facebook where he travels with his bike and customers. Last time I saw him, he was motoring across South Africa, and a month earlier in Laos (where on Earth is Laos?). I would also love to go to South Africa one day – and wouldn't it be nice if someone were paying me to go? I'm so envious!

Lifestyle entrepreneurship means turning your hobby into your work. Work doesn't feel like work because it's your lifestyle. That kind of entrepreneur's life goal is to enjoy life and finance their lifestyle through entrepreneurship.

Living an entrepreneurial life is about setting goals and getting closer to those goals every day. They know what they want, what milestones to set, and measure their progress.

The unstoppable entrepreneur is on their way to a chosen harbour, checking the navigator to see if the course is correct. If they hit a headwind, the unstoppable entrepreneur tackles it.

If there are pirates, they fight or steer clear.

Decide which harbour you want to head toward. And make sure you're on the right course.

> *"You have to be careful what you wish for,*
> *because you may achieve it."*
> Andy McCoy

#13 Be Positive and Enjoy Life

The unstoppable you has a positive attitude towards life. You show gratitude to others and encourage them. You also encourage others by reminding them to say thanks.

It's said that the secret ingredient to Amazon.com's success is the positivity and happiness of Jeff Bezos. He describes himself as being a genuinely positive person. Even his wife says, "If Jeff is unhappy, just wait five minutes".

I've noticed that employees want to work with a leader that thinks positively – a leader who always sees a better future. Happiness and joy is interpreted as 'we're doing good' and we have what it takes to make things better.

On the carousel of success, positivity spins new positivity. Customer success creates entrepreneur success. A smile costs nothing and is also contagious. Say thanks and be encouraging. By choosing a positive style of leadership, you can affect the success of your customers and employees. Be happy. Boost your strengths and cheer on others. Smile! :)

#14 Sleep and Remember to Relax

The unstoppable you remembers to spend time recuperating, because that's how you can achieve greater results. The unstoppable you can't perform well without rest.

I once worked with a super-entrepreneur who put in 20 hours per day. He burned out and his company was destroyed. As it turns out, the super-entrepreneur was not superman.

Another entrepreneur colleague tried to keep going by drinking alcohol – you may guess that this was also not a recipe for success.

You need to rest every night so you're ready for your next day of challenges. Your life is valuable. Take care of yourself. Balance in life is important.

#15 When You Need Help, Call for it

My friend got a letter from a tax officer who said they would file his company into bankruptcy. I'm happy that he called me. We spoke for an hour and a half on the phone discussing his financial situation and the reasons that brought him into trouble. He couldn't talk about his company situation at home, and discussions with his bookkeeper had stopped.

Together, we made an action plan. We chose to discuss the situation with the tax officer. He made a payment plan with the tax office, and a debt of one hundred thousand was corrected to a debt of ten thousand. To pay his loan, he took a new loan from the bank and managed to pay everything.

Remember the people who can help you. There are also public assistance lines and services, or lawyers who can help you in these situations. The only thing you need to do is call for help.

Of course it's very hard to accept your own failure, but it's a bigger problem to never even ask for help. The unstoppable you can admit when you've failed. When you're in trouble, you call for help.

Consider whom you can call on when you need help. And if you need help now, call that person right away!

Create New Competitive Advantages

You should only compete when you have a competitive advantage. That means finding something that's easy for you, but difficult for your competitors.

In sports, one athlete may be good at the 100-meter dash, while another might be better at running marathons. Train in the field that you know you can do and want to be the best.

When your competitors are developing, some of your competitive advantages transform into normal competitive abilities that everyone in your market has. That's when you'll need to find new competitive advantages.

You can find competitive advantages in, for example, continual innovation, personnel attitude, cost structure, location, size of your business, your processes, different pricing, or in your ability to learn new things.

Consider how you can create and find new competitive advantages – the type of advantages that are difficult or impossible for your competitors to copy.

#16 Create a Stable Entrepreneurship Base

The unstoppable entrepreneur makes money, but also collects social, mental, and physical entrepreneurship capital. With that capital they can survive through both challenging and easy markets.

Stability may be built by continual renewal of competitive advantages or through learning new skills, but it's also gained from a diversified portfolio.

I've built my own business group, LavasDesign Ltd., on portfolio thinking, diversification, and by continually growing my companies into a business accelerator cluster. My business cluster is now 10 times bigger than it was 10 years ago, and the amount of employees has grown from less than 10 up to 80 employees currently.

You can renew and rebuild companies through better leadership. Diversification is a known tool in portfolio management, but it's also a way to reduce risk in investments, or in this case, companies. Your ownership base also makes a big difference. By putting together a solid team of entrepreneur colleagues, you can create stability and continuity for your companies.

I changed my "me and my company"-way of thinking to "we and our company and our team"-thinking. My co-entrepreneurs have such unique knowledge that it's difficult to copy. Team entrepreneurship has more power than self-entrepreneurship.

Remember to collect for yourself social, mental and monetary investments, as well as structural stability for your company and entrepreneurship capital.

#17 Choose Your Career Path

The unstoppable entrepreneur never sticks with just one company or position. You go further in your career path.

I started out on my career path as self-employed. A career consultant once told me that the estimated time I can invest in company development is about seven years.

I thought about what I needed to do after those seven years were up. My realisation – I would need to improve and develop myself, and create new entrepreneurial opportunities.

In time, my company grew and I began searching for a follower from within my company that I could trust and transfer my tasks to. Finding the right person to manage the company I established was the only way to scale-up my entrepreneurial career and to make time for expanding our portfolio.

At the same time my company was growing, I also grew professionally: as an entrepreneur, a leader, and as a managing director. It's important to develop from one role to another. At first I was stuck in my old roles, but later I got the courage to delegate everything to my follower.

I continued onward in my career path, and changed focus to another company. We established another company to grow. Others at my first company now had possibilities to grow into leadership. So the second company grew and my colleagues learned to be successful.

I've not yet done any big exits. What I've experienced and described is only one entrepreneurial model. I could, for example, sell companies that I've built and after that start a brand new company. By selling companies at a reasonable price, you can get good seed money to start the next company.

Create a career plan for yourself. Live your career path.

Don't stick to just one thing.

14 April 2012 – Shanghai, China

A tree's branches grow in many directions so that the tree can collect enough sun with its leaves. Its roots also branch out to endure storms and get enough water. The unstoppable entrepreneur secures their own success in a similar way: through a diversified portfolio and a networked business model.

Keep on learning.

18 April 2012 – Bangkok, Thailand

Develop yourself constantly. Take care of your skills and knowledge. Upgrade yourself. Keep on learning. Some knowledge you learn will be outdated in seven years. Some information becomes outdated in just three years. Perpetual learning is important.

#18 Be Proud of Your Professional Skills

Unstoppable entrepreneurship requires a deep respect for yourself and your skills. You must be proud to serve others with the talents and skills you have.

One of my friends is a phenomenal photographer, who's well aware of her talent. She also gets lots of appreciation, endorsements and new orders.

Another friend is an incredibly talented art designer who passionately follows the latest design trends. He gets new orders because old customers recommend him.

A third friend of mine is a talented sales trainer who inspires and motivates salespeople to achieve new top sales. He concentrates on his strengths as a trainer. This friend once told me that leadership in sales means motivating other salespeople to desire success and to win.

Here's another example. While on my trip to Thailand, my birthday came around. I went in for a traditional Thai massage. The masseuse was the oldest I had ever seen – she was clearly very experienced. As she worked, I could sense she truly respected her own professional skills. My experience was unforgettable, and the secret was her deep knowledge and understanding of the human body and muscles.

Respect yourself. Develop your skills constantly. Consider what you'll do when your retirement age grows near. Think about how you can perform in a way that people will recommend your services to others.

#19 Buy More "Lottery Tickets"

The unstoppable entrepreneur knows that having plenty of revenue streams is a good thing. Think of revenue streams as if they were lottery tickets: the probability of success increases when you have more possible ways to be successful.

I have hundreds of customers. Sometimes one orders more, sometimes less. I can serve my customers according to different financial situations. In growing markets some customers may place more orders, whereas others place more orders during recessions.

The amount of customers is important in managing risk and growth. In just a couple years, a small customer of mine became a huge customer. At the same time, a big customer scaled down to become a smaller customer when their business industry was in crisis.

I've made several angel investments in startup businesses, and own small shares in dozens of startups. Some of them have been failures, while some became great successes. From the starting line, you'll never know what opportunities you'll get when you invest in something. You can never be exactly sure what will be successful.

Some businesses I can influence myself, while some I can't. Luck is a happy accident on your way to success. It comes to people who work hard toward their dreams. Luck is the good stuff that happens without planning.

Give yourself the possibility to be lucky with concurring possibilities for success. Make your own luck by moving forward, being curious and working hard. "Buy" more "lottery tickets" in your life.

#20 Your Customer's Success is the No. 1 Priority

The unstoppable entrepreneur only hires world-class people who focus on the success of their customers.

A customers-first mindset requires that the people in your company have it within. You can teach people many things, but a service-centric attitude is something found at your core.

Our staff needs to consider what's best for our customers. We need to help them be successful. When we help them, they will thank us with recurring new orders. In the end, it's the customer's decision whether they place more orders with us or from our competitors.

I've seen many falling stars in my career. Getting your first sale is easy when you over-promise. But if you under-deliver on that first delivery, a second sale is nearly impossible. In every sale it's better to under-promise and over-deliver.

The second sale is challenging. The ones that seal the deal are those who can see the benefits in the long run and work toward the customer's success. Working hard toward your customer's success isn't a sprint to the finish. It's a marathon that requires perpetual work.

Your success is dependent on how you treat your customers. Always prioritise their success first.

#21 Work When There's Work to Be Done

Being unstoppable means understanding you need to sell when your customer wants to buy. I've learned that every business and every product has its time. Professional fishers know you should go fishing early in the morning, because that's the time when you get the best catches.

Everything has its own golden age. The golden age, then, is a unique instance in time when it's possible to do profitable business. It wasn't smart to make petrol until there were cars. Publishing in print became profitable after printing machines, but during the Internet-era, delivery became effective enough that print business started to shrink.

In the 1990s, we had an online portal, artic.net. We had 200,000 unique visitors in Finland alone when there were only about 600,000 total citizens online during that era. Even with so many located in Finland, this business was not profitable. Why? The golden age for portal businesses had not yet emerged in Finland. We tried to sell banner ads, but customers then didn't understand what we were selling. Online business became profitable 10 years later. Nowadays that site could work and even be profitable. Imagine that – we were 15 years ahead of our time! Fortunately, I sold that company and now have other businesses.

Accept that everything has its time. If one business is not working now, it may work later or maybe it just doesn't work any more. If that's the case, adapt – do something else.

Accept that it's only useful to strike when the iron's hot, and know you should back off when it's not. Life is full of possibilities. Choose what is most possible at this moment.

**Life is full of promises.
Keep them.**

6 April 2012 – Rayong, Thailand
Fishermen return from an early start at work fishing all morning.
Photo taken from a 27th-floor balcony.

Lead others

Being unstoppable means leading not only yourself, but also others. Most entrepreneurs start out without any leadership education. But after hiring their first employee, the entrepreneur becomes a boss.

When your amount of personnel is growing, the need for good leadership is most important.

Sooner or later, those entrepreneurs have to hire a professional manager or they need to grow in to leaders themselves.

You can make more time to pursue new challenges only by leading others.

Even if you hire a manager, you need to lead them.

In the following chapters, I'll cover topics related to growth as a leader.

#22 Become a Better Leader

Being unstoppable means improving your skills to make yourself a better leader. Entrepreneurship is not sprint race. It's more like a combination of marathon and orienteering. Sometimes you should stop to check where you are now and decide which direction is best to go. Choosing your direction is leadership.

I noticed quite early on that if I wanted to see my business grow, I had to hire my first employee. Soon after, I noticed that I needed other team members to become partners in the company.

I had no business or leadership education when I started my first company out of high school. Soon, I had 17 people working at my company, so I was forced to grow as a leader. I joined JCI and I started to study for an MBA while I was running my company.

I've learned that being a leader and entrepreneur is about sharing your vision, knowing where you are and setting goals with your team. The leader gives some perspective, while also discovering new insights from within the team.

Leadership and management are about making choices. It's about showing by example and making things apparent to your employees.

The unstoppable entrepreneur leads their company in such a way that business never stops – even when the entrepreneur isn't around.

Companies require dynamic managing directors and a board that deliberates on the issues that matter. Companies need people who can think about their clients, who want to train their skills, and have the passion to make business processes better.

Build your organisation so it becomes unstoppable. Grow as a leader.

#23 Hire Only World-Class People

At only 17 years old, I was one of the best web designers in Finland – not to mention the world. I didn't have very specialised programming skills, so I hired my first employee and brought new world-class skills into my company. We were an efficient pair and we made a lot of things together.

Someone once gave me some advice that you should hire better professionals than yourself. When our business blossomed and the dot-com hype in the 2000s blinded me, I unfortunately forgot that good advice. We started hiring people who didn't have top-notch skills – too many juniors who required a senior's help.

When the dot-com bubble burst in 2001, we had to downsize our business. We still had work for all the world-class people, but we had to let go of the juniors and the mediocre employees. Unfortunately, I also had to lay off some awesome people, but our company survived.

These days I always remember that golden rule about hiring world-class people. I try to remind our people about personal development and perpetual learning. Our customers appreciate our strong professional skills and I'm proud of my colleagues and employees. Put the best people to the best places so they can show and shine their best.

Hire experts that add new skills to your own skills. Find better professionals than yourself. Bring in people you can trust and to whom you can easily delegate responsibilities.

29 March 2012 – Bokor Mountain, Cambodia

At Bokor Mountain, I thought about the importance of professional skills and personal development to company success, and happiness in work. And I wrote about personal development and hiring only world-class people.

#24 Assemble a Team That Wants to Grow

Growth is a strategic choice. If you don't want to grow your company, skip this chapter and go directly to the next. But remember to stop back here when you're ready to grow again.

That said, the unstoppable entrepreneur does want to grow their company at some point. Unstoppable entrepreneurship is knowing that founding a 20 M revenue company is not much more difficult than a 1 M revenue company. To be unstoppable, you gather a team, investors and management who all want growth.

Research shows that growth companies are run by a team of, on average, five entrepreneurs. In software entrepreneurship, research found that one ultimate reason for growth is the team's enthusiasm for it. The board, management and investors should all be focused on growth.

A growing company needs a strong growth strategy and world-class vision. If you want to achieve this, you need to measure your progress at the board level.

Growth is also dependent on the field of business you're in. It's easier to grow when you're in an expanding industry. If your business domain is shrinking, you may find it nearly impossible to grow organically.

Your business can only grow when you want to make it happen. Consider what possibilities you have for business growth. If you can't find any, shut down your impossible-to-grow business and start a new one that you know you can nurture.

#25 Benchmark Your Business Against the Best in the World

The unstoppable entrepreneur wants to create a world-class company. Therefore, we cannot compare our companies to mediocre ones, but only to the best of the world and to the best in other business areas.

While I was in Thailand, I got bit by a wild dog and had to go to hospital. There was a nurse waiting for me at reception. She quickly tested my blood pressure and asked what happened. Her assistant entered my personal information into an e-patient card on her tablet. It was effective and excellent customer service.

We then moved into the emergency room where they measured my weight. The nurse directed me to a bed and started to disinfect the dog bite. Immediately after the dog bite was cleaned, a doctor came in.

He asked what vaccinations I had. In my home country, Finland, rabies is not a problem, so I didn't have any protection against it. The doctor suggested I get the Rabies vaccine because dogs in Thailand may be infected.

He wrote the orders with his tablet directly into my e-patient card. Afterward, the nurse gave me the necessary vaccinations. I got some medicines and left the hospital – easy as that.

The whole process was much faster than I have yet seen in any other country. Still – they could perhaps improve it by comparing their processes to those of a Formula 1 pit stop. Think about it – could you compare your own business to other businesses in other countries or even a different business industry?

#26 Sell When it's Time to Sell

The unstoppable entrepreneur has a sixth sense for understanding customer needs. Sometimes your customers don't even know that they want to buy something. Provide the proverbial "itch to scratch".

When I was in Shanghai, a pirate-products saleswoman took me through a secret corridor comprised of carton packages. It looked like a dead end, but when she knocked a secret code on the wall, a secret door opened.

We came into a small shop through the door, which was masked to look like a shelf on the other side. The shop was full of pirate goods. They kept the shop hidden because in China it's illegal to sell pirate goods, and if the police are not corrupt, they can throw you into jail. On that day the area was heavily policed, so they had to be even more careful.

I'm not a shopaholic, so it's usually quite impossible to sell me anything. I didn't know if I even wanted to buy anything there, and I don't even like to buy pirate products anyway. But the point of this story is that this shop, with its secret corridors, was so exciting and cool that I was compelled to buy something. So she persuaded me even though I didn't know I wanted to buy something. I bought a pirated wallet as a travel gift for myself. I've never used that wallet, but maybe my deal kept one or two Chinese people employed for a short time.

There's that old saying, "when in Rome, do as the Romans do". Should we consider this as part of doing business abroad? If we're in China, should we act according to the local customs? Are we trying too hard to work under our own cultural rules and expectations? Is there something we could learn from other cultures?

Sell when it's time to sell. Your customer may not know yet that they want to buy. Consider if there are other cultural norms that could help you conduct your business.

23.4.2012 Shanghai, China.
Your customer may not know yet that they want to buy.

#27 Look from Different Perspectives

Being unstoppable means changing your perspective when necessary. When something looks too immense to handle, I play a little mind trick and try to imagine the situation from a skyscraper's perspective. I basically use my imagination to perceive things from a customer's or competitor's point of view.

Take, for example, how your perspective on two different buildings changes based on where you're looking from. At ground level, a 50-floor building appears very tall. In Shanghai, I went to the top of a 100-floor building. Up there, everything looked different – a 50-floor building was now smaller. And if I were to take a helicopter and fly up even higher, both buildings would look smaller.

My friend's son is an enthusiastic mountain biker. One day we wanted to buy one of the boy's old bikes, but he said he didn't want to sell it. His father saw things from a different angle and said, "Look around, son. You have four bikes and you want a new one. You need to let go of something". The boy decided his father was right, and sold his bike to us after all.

Like this boy that needed a fresh perspective from his father, the unstoppable entrepreneur needs mentors and assistants. Together they can examine what's important and determine how to prioritise.

Perceiving the world from outside ourselves helps us find the right perspective. Examine things from different angles and perspectives. And try to put yourself into your customer's shoes.

Shanghai World Financial Center (SWFC), China

When you look at 20-floor buildings from a 100-floor building, they look very small.

#28 Don't Lead an Industry You Don't Understand

The unstoppable entrepreneur wants to be a part of businesses that they completely understand and know how to lead. I've been involved in several business acquisitions and exits. The best of those business transfers were fully understood by both the buyer and seller. Only when you intimately know every issue within your company, you can optimise and lead the business.

According to ownership change research, business transfers are most successful when the company traded is something the buyer already knows how to lead. Those businesses help the buyer establish in new geographic areas and attract new skills into the company.

Conversely, the worst business transfer cases are those in which the buyer tries to leap into an industry they don't fully understand.

The best managers and leaders I know understand their business inside and out. This allows them to be well organised and stay focused on the right things. A leader with a complete grasp on their industry can see aspects of their business that others can't pick up on.

Think about what type of business you can lead. Concentrate on your strengths. Do what you are good at, where you're good at it. Take yourself and your skills where they're needed. Network in places where you'll find the expertise you're lacking. And steer clear of businesses you don't understand.

#29 Prioritise and Recognise What's Most Important

The unstoppable entrepreneur has often started at a small business. During their adventures, the business has grown. We get customers who are viable to our business. At some point we find ourselves in a situation that some customers or revenue streams don't fit with our other businesses, and are difficult to execute or no longer profitable.

Prioritisation means putting thing in order. Who do you serve first? Who is the most important customer? If both a big and small customer want jobs done by tomorrow, which one do you serve first?

You need to prioritise in your business, but also in your private life. How do you spend your time? Where do you advertise? Are you going to a seminar to learn how to sell, or do you go out and practice sales in real-life situations with your customers?

When you prioritise your own time, remember to reserve some time for renewing your skills, creativity and rest. Set aside time for learning and studying, but also enough time for the productive work that pays your salary.

Prioritise and decide what's truly important. When you have too many things on your task list, you need to know where to start. Which tasks are getting you closer to your dreams? What tasks cannot be left undone?

On the next page, note how easy it is to lose sight of the children if you stare too long at all the colourful balls. Are there one or two kids here?

22 April 2012 –
In the ball pit with my sons

An entrepreneur may relax but never stops thinking. Even when I'm on vacation, I let my mind work with different scenarios and plan the future.

#30 Develop Your Team's Skills

An unstoppable company has many opportunities to learn. When people are more enthusiastic about their work, they're more effective. If you have the desire and will to learn and develop, you stay in better shape and are more competitive.

Put your team to work together – let them learn from each other. When their professional skills further develop, your ability to compete grows.

There are no stupid questions. At work, many people say, "Yes, I can". We too often expect that professionals know everything. When some professionals face new terms, ideas or challenges, they're too proud to express that they don't know enough. They may be afraid to ask the "stupid questions".

I've noticed that if leaders start asking those "stupid questions", people relax and begin asking more themselves. Problems get solved faster. New lessons may often be closer than you know.

I'm partner and founder of W3 Group Finland. W3 is a founder member in the programming language community, PHP User Group Finland. I believe that by supporting the PHP community and its users, we can also help our own company stay ahead in PHP development.

Seek out new ways to learn or find new opportunities for your team to grow. Learning new skills and knowledge makes your team and company stronger.

22 April 2012 – Zhujiajiao Water Town, China

Signs in multiple languages. Speak your customer's language.

#31 Keep Your Eyes Open and Stay At the Leading Edge

The unstoppable entrepreneur fuels their brain with news and important industry information. I visited China and to my surprise, I noticed how quickly the world changes. Chinese people work fast. They're so fast that China will soon surpass the USA as an economical power.

If you're in China, you may notice that there's a lot of competition everywhere. The Chinese want to be best at school, best at work and they want their children to be successful. In more developed countries, we are more satisfied with our lives, and we don't feel the need to compete so much anymore. But if we pause in our own personal development, we also stop developing our teams, our companies and our countries.

I prefer that we benchmark ourselves against the harsh competitive culture in China. There are some negatives to this way of life, but there are also many good things we can learn from the Chinese. Globalisation has transformed business, and now nearly all industries compete worldwide. If we want to be the world's best, we need to be better than the Chinese. We need to understand how fast they are and need to improve ourselves at an even faster pace.

Measure your competitive level in the entrepreneurial world championships by benchmarking your own abilities and skills against the best in the world. You need to be ready to realise if you're in world-class shape or not. If you're not in world-class condition, you won't manage in global competition – you'll need to start training for speed. Only perpetual training makes you the world's fastest.

Follow the world's development and trends. Stay conscious about how fast or slow your global competitors are. For that's the only way to stay on top of your competition.

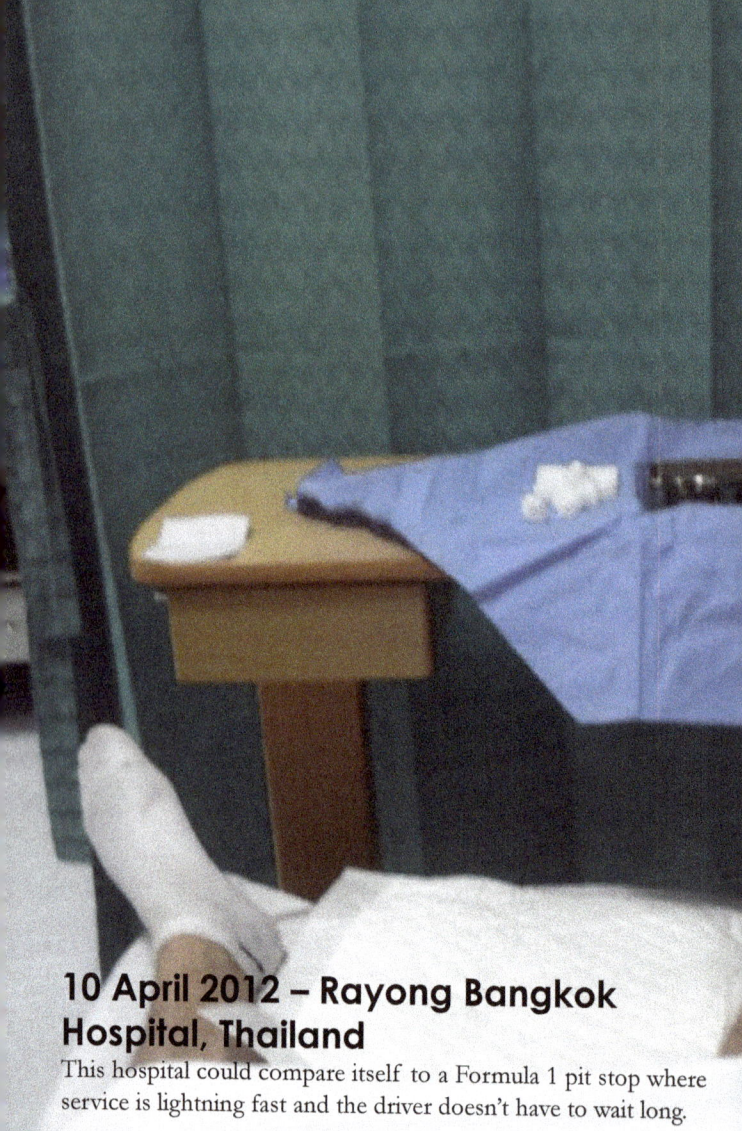

10 April 2012 – Rayong Bangkok Hospital, Thailand

This hospital could compare itself to a Formula 1 pit stop where service is lightning fast and the driver doesn't have to wait long.

#32 Create a Successful Ecosystem

The unstoppable entrepreneur is successful, because they want to help others thrive. Hwang and Horowitt studied successful companies and what they noticed was that these companies also create successful ecosystems around them. The researchers compare successful ecosystems to biological ecosystems such as a rainforest, where animals and plants live in symbiosis to give each other space to live, safety and energy.

A successful ecosystem means people are innovating together. Many new startups have sprung up due to our ecosystem. We spread and get ideas. New and awesome ideas are born when people inspire each other – when we help others find new innovations and success stories.

People often ask me where they could buy this or that, and I like to recommend entrepreneurs who have served me well. Their willingness to serve and help me be successful makes me want to recommend them to others. And I know that in turn, they will also be served and helped to be successful.

Consider how can you facilitate your environment and network to be successful. Help your network and ecosystem thrive and you'll be blessed in return with success.

#33 Train Your Body

The unstoppable entrepreneur never stops striving for achievements. They're either recreating an earlier successful event or are preparing for the next top event.

For top athletes, preparation means better endurance, strength and power. If an athlete stops training, their muscles start to shrink and their stomach gets bigger.

The same thing happens to an entrepreneur if they're not continually training. The entrepreneur has to discuss and learn new skills. We also need to try new challenges and take care of our physical health.

The summer of 2013 was a failure for me. I was lazy all summer. I didn't take my weekly time for sport. I was eating poorly and drinking too much. After that summer I was more tired than ever, and I needed more sleep than usual. I wasn't in very good shape.

When I started working out again, I immediately noticed how bad my physical condition had become. I became exhausted very quickly. After one month of training, I got back on my wellness track. When I skipped physical training, my mental health suffered immediately and my work performance weakened.

Keeping yourself in good physical shape is extremely important. The old proverb, "A healthy mind in a healthy body" is often more true than we know.

Life is a challenge – face it. Keep your eyes on your physical and mental health. Hire a personal trainer and stay in good shape.

#34 Live For the Moment, But Keep Your Eyes on the Future

The unstoppable entrepreneur is not afraid of change. They keep their eye on the company's long-term goals, but at the same time, live for the moment and prioritise tasks for this week and today.

They can even make big decisions because they know that those decisions will help us be successful in the long run. Being unstoppable means seeing change as a possibility to create something new.

The unstoppable entrepreneur wants to live every moment in life to the fullest, never forgetting why they started their business. Enthusiasm for making the world better, a passion for competition and world-class success are the drivers that keep them on the move.

Moore and Noyce founded Intel to make memory chips. The Japanese price war triggered them to search for better businesses, so they, along with Andy Grove, founded a new business in manufacturing microprocessors. IKEA's Ivar Kamprad started his career by selling pens door to door. We all start somewhere and end up somewhere else. The most important part of the word "startup" is "start".

W3 Group Finland is one of my companies. I founded it when I was just 17 years old. We've learned new technologies and processes over the past 18 years, and we continue to learn from and teach each other. We train new techniques and industry best practices. We've changed our tools and programming frameworks over the years, but noticed there's always a need for software development.

The unstoppable you has courage to make small changes and the ability to stay focused on a long-term vision. Being unstoppable means you know the path is right and the goal is bright.

Life is a game, play it.
6 April 2012 – Canopy adventures Rayong, Thailand
When you're riding a zip-line over the trees, you'd best keep your eyes ahead if you want to brake in time.

#35 Set Measurable Milestones

The unstoppable entrepreneur measures everything. They communicate milestones in a way that people can understand, and give feedback on how to proceed.

We had a "name and number" campaign in one of my companies. Every employee, of course, has their name, but also a number that they had to achieve every day. Numeric values are metrics that people can use to measure their success. Measurement through this campaign helped people clarify their roles. Everyone knew what was expected of them. Of course it was not as simple as this, but you get the idea.

In another company we measure the amount of billable hours. That's what keeps the business profitable. We also measure personal development with a scorecard and customer feedback.

Metrics are important. People focus on things that bring better results. But sometimes metrics are misleading. They may only show perhaps 90% of the truth. Still, I believe that's better than not having any metrics at all. What you measure is what you'll get.

Understandable milestones are important in management. An unstoppable company shares a vision and a clearly marked path. Therefore, people like to work with an unstoppable entrepreneur.

Think about how you could gauge yourself, your tasks, your progress and others. Set milestones and measure them. Tell people what the numbers are and how you know your employees have succeeded.

Bokor Mountain, Cambodia

At Bokor Mountain, I thought about leaving a legacy and wondering about my 180-year plan. I also thought about my friends who are in the process of selling their business and what I would do in a similar situation.

#36 Express Your Goals as a Share-holder. Show Your Will as the Owner.

One of the most important tasks of both small and large company owners is to show which direction you want the company to go.

Others expect me to tell them how I want my company to develop. Do I want growth or profitability? They want to know in which areas should we focus, how much I believe we can grow this year, or if the business is potentially shrinking. Employees want me to show how much I believe we can make in revenue or profit.

Often the will of the owner is unclear. But the owner has a lot of power, and that power can and should be used. You can employ that power to make your business develop as you want, but you need to tell people what your expectations are.

As an entrepreneur, I can take risks that may appear very crazy to others. From my point of view, I think those risks are worth taking and I know how to handle them if those risks come into play.

If the direction doesn't look right, but you're certain you need to change direction, do it. Challenge your employees to rethink. Be bold and ask questions that others hesitate to ask. But don't change direction too often, because otherwise your people will get confused.

When others understand why your vision and will is right, stick to it. That's the way to proceed.

Your job is to tell employees where they need to focus and what's important. Create an inspiring vision. Be enthusiastic. Spread your enthusiasm. Show direction and express your goals as an owner.

22 April 2012 – Shanghai World Financial Center (SWFC), China

It's almost impossible to imagine a 100-storey building if you've never before seen anything like it. How many people can fit inside? It must have been a fascinating building project to be part of.

#37 Money is a Tool, Not a Goal

The unstoppable entrepreneur uses money like an investor. Money is not a goal – it's a tool to grow business. For many startups, this is easy to understand. For some well-financed startups or children who inherited a company, it may be a difficult concept to understand.

Many family businesses have gone down the path where the first generation establishes the company, the second generation makes it grow, and the third generation ends up destroying it. Unfortunately, business transfers from generation to generation are often a disaster. It's generally smarter to just leave the children a huge amount of inheritance money than it is to transfer over the company.

Is it even necessary for a company to live forever? An unstoppable entrepreneur plays their role like an investor. From the investor's point of view, the company is built to make money. And money is a tool to make more money. As an owner, the unstoppable entrepreneur makes sure the company's value constantly grows.

In Asia they have a principle: get wealthy, but slowly. In the Nordic countries, where I live, we say: keep your assets in good condition, and leave them in better condition than when you got them for the next generation.

If you inherited company stocks, keep them in good condition and develop the company further. If you don't know how, hire a manager who's better than you. Hire someone who can take care of your valuable company. If you can't find a good manager, sell the company to someone who can take care of it. I've noticed that it's better to spend only the money that you've earned yourself.

It's difficult to leave inheritance. You never know how your kids or their kids will treat your wealth. When you're gone, you can't tell them what to do with it, nor teach them anymore.

It's easier to leave material wealth and money behind. We can't take anything with us when we leave this planet. If you don't want to leave your company for your kids, consider if you could sell the company to your employees. Think about it – maybe there's someone inside your company who would like to take over?

Many entrepreneurs who are already 55 years old don't even think about transferring their company to the next generation. The process takes many years, so that's why you should think about these issues yourself.

You may pass on money and shares, but inheritance also includes life lessons and heritage: how to live a good life and how to raise kids. You've got the precious gift of life, so take good care of it and pass it on. Make sure that your kids have opportunities that are at least as good as yours, both materially and emotionally.

#38 Live for the Moment

Time goes by. Can you hear it?
Now. Now. Now. Now.
Not when you retire. Now.
Not soon. Now.
Not only on Fridays. Now.
Not in the evening. Now

The unstoppable entrepreneur lives for the moment, enjoying life with all its flavour. All good and bad moments are part of a good life. You can always learn from failures – learn to enjoy them and call them experiences. Fail forward and learn from it.

Remember to dream. Remind yourself about great moments. Enjoy the moment you're in as if this were the best thing that ever happened to you.

Think about all the things you could still experience. If you came to this moment through a mess of obstacles, don't build new ones in front of you. Build yourself a life of dreams. And move closer toward your dreams everyday.

If the day feels boring, accept it. There are some people who can't even sense boredom. And if you feel like your day is difficult, remember that someone else is surely going through much harder times.

If you love your life, enjoy it to its fullest. Share the joy with others. If you're happy, spread it all around. Call a friend and delight their day.

Smile now. Lift your thumbs up. And enjoy the moment.

Ilkka O. Lavas

Life is beautiful, admire it.

#39 Unstoppable Thanks

I want to wish a very special thanks to my family for the awesome trip to Asia. Without that experience, I probably couldn't have written this book. We're born with two ears and one mouth so we can listen twice as much as we speak. I also wish to thank my company partners and employees. Thanks for the possibility to travel to Asia to write this book. Thanks to my mentors and colleagues for your time. Thanks to everyone who shared ideas and articles through social media. Thanks for sharing and the great discussions.

Sources for inspiration

While writing this book, I've found inspiration, ideas, thoughts and encouragement from many awesome people whom I respect. A warm thanks to: Jukka Niemelä, Linda Sandoval, F. Peter Cuneo, Satu Vainio, Taneli Tikka, Matias Savolainen, Terhi Majasalmi, Anthony De Mello, Kemopetrol, Ollis Leppänen, Ville Lähdesmäki, Teemu Arina, Martti Laosmaa, Kirsti Lonka, Peter F. Drucker, Jussi T. Koski, The Dalai Lama, Mihaly Csikszentmihalyi, Esa Saarinen, Jukka Hassinen, Mother Teresa, Susanna Rantanen, Jukka Hietanen, Severi Virolainen, Aki Antman, Stephen R. Covey, Eero Lehti, Chisu, Jussi Muurikainen, Hjallis Harkimo, Niko Papula, Juha Viitala, Saara Liukkonen, Hanna Mäenpää, Lauri, Katja Ståhl, Riitta Saarikangas, Juha Koponen, Kyösti Kakkonen, and all of you who have helped me during my career whose name doesn't fit on this page.

And a special thanks to my mentors, coaches, business partners, friends at work, customers, relatives and co-operative partners.

Author

Ilkka O. Lavas

Ilkka is a 35-year-old serial entrepreneur in the ICT and Media industries from Finland. Lavas started his entrepreneurial adventures at 17 years old in high school, and now employs nearly 100 people in his companies. He's given talks about entrepreneurial attitude for thousands of people. His blog is used for entrepreneurial education in Finland. This is his third book.

www.ilkkaolavas.com

SaaraLiu

SaaraLiu (Saara Liukkonen) is an energetic Scandinavian designer and entrepreneur. It was SaaraLiu's idea to design this book so small that it could neatly fit into your back pocket. She's been involved in company marketing and design for 20 years.

www.saaraliu.fi

Recommended Self Help and Self-Management Books

Jonathan Livingston Seagull, by Richard Bach
The 7 Habits of Highly Effective People, by Stephen R. Covey
Know Can Do!, by Paul J. Meyer
Profiles of Success, by Paul J. Meyer
Managing Performing Living, by Fredmund Malik
The Fifth Discipline: The Art and Practice of the Learning Organization, by Peter Senge
Goals!, by Brian Tracy
Trust Capital: the Third Force of Entrepreneurship, by Ensio Miettinen
Getting Things Done, by David Allen
Awaken the Giant Within, by Tony Robbins
Get the Edge, by Tony Robbins
Steve Jobs, by Walter Isaacson
Good to Great, by Jim Collins

"An interesting, understandable and deep book. Every page has something interesting to learn."

> Jussi T. Koski, Professor of Education,
> University of Helsinki

"Ilkka writes about entrepreneurship straight from his heart and backed by strong experience. The findings in this book are useful for international businesses."

> Jari Soini, Director,
> Cybercom China

"Thanks for the interesting book. I enjoyed reading it. You have the right attitude about entrepreneurship!"

> Kyösti Kakkonen,
> CEO, Tokmanni

"The world needs new entrepreneurs. This book truly captures a young entrepreneur's passion and his ponderings on life values."

> Juha Koponen,
> Managing Director, Veikkaus Oyj

My own notes

www.ingramcontent.com/pod-product-compliance
Lightning Source LLC
Chambersburg PA
CBHW051227120626
46547CB00013B/1547